A Complete Primer on the
Causes and Treatment of
Seasonal Affective Disorder (S.A.D.)

Banishing The Blues
of
Seasonal Affective Disorder

Published By The Indoor Sun Shoppe Corp.

The information in this book is true and complete to the best of our knowledge. All recommendations are made without guarantee on the part of the author. The author and publisher disclaim any liability in connection with the use of this information.

Illustrations: Doug Ready
Edited by: Andrew Engelson

All Inquiries to The Indoor Sun Shoppe   911 N.E. 45th Seattle Wa. 98105
(206) 634-3727

For Product Information
www.indoorsun.com

Printed in the U.S.A.   ISBN 0-9677416-0-2

Acknowledgments

The author would like to thank Steve Murphy, who was the primary inspiration for the development of this project. Thanks also, to Shaun Murphy for his tremendous expertise in the mechanics of publication. Appreciation goes to the crew at the Indoor Sun Shoppe for their support and expertise in bringing joyful and healthful light to people all year long.

Table of Contents

Author's Foreword

With this publication, it is our purpose to give the reader a working overview of the causes, symptoms, and the application of light therapy to alleviate the depression associated with Seasonal Affective Disorder (S.A.D.). This book aims to provide a concise survey of the relevant medical literature, popular publications, personal interviews and anecdotes, product descriptive material, and almost two decades of experience in the design and use of light therapy in the treatment of what was known in the beginning only as the "winter blues."

Through diligent work by a number of dedicated medical professionals, Seasonal Affective Disorder—with its array of bothersome and often debilitating symptoms—has been clearly defined and presented to practitioners and the public at large. It is the purpose of this book to aid the reader in self-education about S.A.D. It is not intended to replace the considered opinion of qualified medical professionals. Indeed, it is hoped that the reader, once having identified potential S.A.D. symptoms, will seek trained clinical expertise. With a doctor's help, one can work to create a successful treatment plan that may use phototherapy in conjunction with all other appropriate measures.

We have shared the struggle to banish the "winter blues" brought about by what we now know as S.A.D., and it is our sincere hope that this book may help the reader start out on the path to a happier, healthier, and more productive life.

Bruce Charles Barr
Author

The Downside of Moving On Up

As mankind enters the twenty-first century, in spite of all his creativity and technical innovation, he remains, at the core, a creature still biologically and physiologically programmed by his development in the equitorial regions. The spread of civilization into higher latitudes is relatively recent when compared to the span of man's time on the planet. Much more recent still, have been dramatic advances in the complexity of social structures and the modes of modern life.

These complexities provide many obvious benefits to man's health and welfare. Yet, this rapid change from a simple hunting and gathering culture whose activity cycles were set by the natural rhythms of the tropical day and night to a world-spanning twenty-four hour-a-day high tech society has produced stresses on the human organism that it is ill-equipped to handle. There has simply not been enough time for evolutionary accommodation to mankind's geographical spread and cultural advances.

One such negative consequence, only recently formally recognized by the medical field, is associated with living in higher latitudes with their short, dark winter days. This is exacerbated by lives spent mostly indoors with little exposure to strong natural light. The resulting mood disorder is one in which symptoms of depression start as the days grow shorter and increase as winter deepens...and relief only comes with the longer and brighter days of spring.

Seasonal Affective Disorder (or S.A.D.) is a unique

depression syndrome resulting in dramatic changes in otherwise healthy and happy people. Normally energetic and productive people feel lethargic and restless. Their concentration lags and productivity drops. Projects and commitments can slip further and further behind; leading occasionally to feelings of failure and low self-esteem. The tiniest of setbacks or stresses may result in long periods of self-doubt and lowered expectations. Interpersonal relationships, never easy to deal with in these fast-paced times, might become more difficult and complicated and sexual interest may fade. Some women experience increased discomfort in their monthly cycles.

In most cases, the S.A.D. sufferer feels an overwhelming need for long periods of sleep and an inability to wake up rested and prepared for the coming day. Frequently, instead of the expected loss of appetite associated with many forms of depression, he or she develops a craving for starchy and sweet foods that may result in overeating and weight gain.

While mankind's biology has brought upon him the misery of Seasonal Affective Disorder...his intelligence and perseverance are now helping him find the way to banish it.

The What, When and Where
of Seasonal Affective Disorder (S.A.D.)

Since the beginning of recorded history, man has exhibited changes in mood and energy as the seasons follow their yearly march. Most people note moderate changes in their mood and reactions over the course of the year. But a small yet significant number of people suffer a clearly pathological and life-altering pattern of problems associated with the coming of winter. For centuries, physicians have observed this phenomenon, but it was not until the 1930s that medical doctors—in conjunction with the newly developing profession of psychology—began to formally make the connection between their patients' onset of depression and the shortening of daylight. Using the limited pharmaceuticals available in that time—in conjunction with the new science of classical psychotherapy—doctors did their best to boost their patients' spirits and energy levels. Having made the connection between the failing light and the onset of symptoms, European physicians became especially concerned with providing a higher quality and quantity of light to their patients. They recommended not only vacations in the lighter and warmer climes of Southern Europe and Northern Africa (for those who could afford them) but exposure to full-body "light baths."

However, it was not until the late 1970s and early 1980s that a few physicians and researchers focused on defining the criteria to be included in the diagnosis of Seasonal Affective Disorder (S.A.D.), searching for the biological and physiological underpinnings of S.A.D., and arriving at possible treatment strategies for it. Only in 1987 did the American Psychiatric Association recognize a version of S.A.D. in its diagnostic manual, the DSM-III-R.

What is S.A.D.?

In deciding whether one indeed suffers from S.A.D., it is best to refer to the definition of S.A.D. outlined by one of the most prominent pioneers in the field—Norman E. Rosenthal, M.D., of the National Institute of Mental Health. Rosenthal described the onset of S.A.D. as at least one major episode of depression in at least two succeeding year's fall-winter period, with an intervening spring and summer during which the symptoms of depression were clearly relieved. This pattern must however exist in the absence of any other clearly defined mood pathology or depression from other identifiable causes.

Symptoms of depression associated with S.A.D. include, but are not limited to:
- Decreases in activity
- Mood changes:
  Increased sadness
  Higher irritability
  Greater anxiety
- Appetite changes:
  Craving of sweets
  Craving of carbohydrates
- Weight increases
- Sleep changes:
  Earlier onset
  Longer duration
  Lower quality of rest
- Daytime tiredness
- Worktime problems

• Social and interpersonal strain
• Menstrual difficulties
• Depression lifts with movement
  toward equator or onset of spring

A series of studies has clearly shown that the predicted pattern and prevalence of S.A.D. sufferers increases according to the subject's distance from the Equator. While S.A.D. may only exist full-blown in fewer than 2 percent of people in Florida, it may occur in 10 percent or more of the population in latitudes comparable to Minnesota. Other regions susceptible to S.A.D. are places that may not be suspect alone by their distance north or south of the Equator, but which have unusual weather conditions that frequently occlude the sun's rays. Examples include foggy San Francisco or the chronically overcast city of Lima in Peru's highlands. Even the dark, unnatural "canyons" of big cities such as New York can replicate the reduced light levels of northern zones.

In addition to those who suffer from clinically significant S.A.D., up to 20 percent of the residents of latitudes above 45° show indications of enough S.A.D.-like symptoms to be considered "subsyndromal" and thus are still likely to benefit from attention. Adding both the S.A.D. and subsyndromal groups represents an estimated 20 percent of the United States' population. This is a large number in itself, but it is certainly dwarfed by the number of people around the world who live in regions sufficiently distant from the equatorial regions to be affected by S.A.D. It is clear that S.A.D. is a problem for millions of people.

S.A.D. in Children and Young Adults

Interviews with adult S.A.D. patients show, not surprisingly, that their symptoms have been with them since youth. They lacked attention in class, did not follow through on schoolwork and showed increased irritability during the winter months.

Researchers have noted that while relatively few children (about 1 percent) exhibit severe problems associated with S.A.D., the numbers jump to around 5 percent upon onset of puberty—suggesting at least some connection to the changes happening at that time in cyclical hormone levels. Studies have also shown that a larger number of girls than boys report symptoms.

It is important to remember that attributing the many ever-changing moods and activities of children to S.A.D. is difficult unless one focuses on the defining clue—a marked change in mood and behavior directly connected to the changes in season and repeated year after year. It is up to parents and caretakers to look for the following symptoms before suspecting the child has S.A.D.:

• Complaints of chronic tiredness
• Rages and temper tantrums
• Difficulty in completing schoolwork
• Slipping grades
• Withdrawal from favorite activities
• Nonspecific physical complaints
• Dramatic craving for junk food

Again, because the above circumstances are not at all unique to the circumstances of S.A.D., it is critical to closely observe how these symptoms coincide with seasonal changes. It is interesting to note that in this day of extreme family mobility and the frequency with which children are subjected to a move to another part of the country, a child may be exposed to many more than one set of winter or low light conditions. High school and college counselors have increasingly noted the effects of S.A.D. upon students who move from more southern climates to be educated under the darker skies of the northern states. Initial findings strongly suggest that the proper geographical location for a school may go far in ameliorating the already considerable stress attendant with starting school in a new place. An extraordinary new set of studies has shown a direct link between levels of light intensity in the school environment and academic performance.

S.A.D. in Seniors

As the population ages, greater and greater consideration for the specific physical and emotional needs of the senior citizenry has developed. The question of depression in elderly populations is now receiving deserved attention, as well as the shift in sleep patterns often observed in the later years of life. The mechanisms affecting sleep patterns, alertness and cognition in seniors are currently being explored. Researchers (especially those doing work in the retirement areas of Florida and the Southwest) report an alleviation of depression symptoms in the elderly due to geographical relocation, even when corrected for other more obvious changes in lifestyle. Not surprisingly, studies in populations of otherwise healthy seniors in San Diego have shown that those who spend more time out in the sunshine report higher levels of personal happiness and absence of depression's symptoms. Indeed, a correlation has been made between the amount of fall and winter darkness the seniors were exposed to and the depth of their level of depression due to S.A.D. for that year.

S.A.D. in Women

While studies of the incidence of S.A.D. in the adult female population are not yet conclusive—and surveys of Iceland and other Nordic populations suggest otherwise—in the United States, women do appear to be more vulnerable than men to the symptoms of S.A.D. Researchers have posited that, since the effects of S.A.D.-associated symptoms seem to peak during the reproductive years and statistically revert to match the level of men in later years, the cyclical secretion of female hormones may play a factor. The question is just now being seriously studied, as are other genetic and developmental factors, such as how body structure and heredity contribute to a person's vulnerability to S.A.D.

S.A.D. and Alcoholism

Most recent research data collected in the northwest United States suggests that the depression connected with S.A.D. may be related to the depression associated with alcoholism. When researchers noticed that some alcoholics experience seasonal fluctuations in the severity of their disease, it was hypothesized that some of the mechanisms that promote the onset of S.A.D. in the general population were underlying this craving for alcohol. Just as there appears to be a familial link to alcoholism, there also seems to be a relationship between S.A.D. and alcoholism in families. As the incidence of S.A.D. increases with latitude, so generally does the incidence of alcoholism. This may reach beyond simply differences in social drinking patterns around the country and between cultures. It has been suggested that because alcohol is a carbohydrate, it may be effective in quickly increasing serotonin levels in the brain and thus act like the family of antidepressants that are used to treat S.A.D. and other depressions. Taken together, the incidence of S.A.D. and alcoholism in some patients makes it likely that treating the associated conditions of S.A.D may prevent relapses in abstinent alcoholics.

S.A.D. and Bipolar Disorder, Bulimia Nervosa and Nonseasonal Depression

In studies of patients with bipolar disorder, bulimia nervosa, and classic non-seasonal depression, it was found that changes in the season appear to have some effect. Manic phases in bipolar disorder may be more frequent in summer months. Some patients show a greater stability of moods when their light-dark schedules are more regulated and predictable. A small amount of research suggests that the disorder may be in some way linked to rapid recycling of circadian rhythms—a phenomenon that is described in greater detail later in this book.

Patients suffering from the bingeing and purging of bulimia nervosa show a definite seasonal pattern to the intensity of their problems. But connecting this phenomenon to S.A.D. is still in the very early stages of research. While typical depression patients do not exhibit the hypersomnia (excessive need for sleep) and eating patterns associated with S.A.D., some do during the winter. This leads some clinicians to believe that people who have what appears to be non-seasonal depression may also have an overlay of S.A.D.

Why S.A.D. Happens

In an organism so complex as the human body, with its multiple and highly interactive systems and pathways, it is to be expected that finding one simple cause for the variety of symptoms associated with S.A.D. would be difficult at best. There is presently, even among the most respected of researchers, no absolute agreement on the mechanisms causing the S.A.D. phenomenon. However, in their continuing pursuit to clarify the biological basis for the symptoms of S.A.D., there is general agreement on several theories. Recent experimental results are encouraging.

The Melatonin Question

One of the primary and most dramatic symptoms of S.A.D. is the need for extending the length of the sleep period, especially much later than usual in the morning hours. Science has long known of the connection between increased levels of the hormone melatonin and periods of sleep. It was a natural jump to explore how levels of melatonin (which is produced in the pineal gland, a small coned-shaped body located in the brain) vary during a mammal's daily sleep and wakefulness cycle. During the 1960s, researchers studying rats were able to stimulate activity in the pineal gland by exposing the animals to intense light.

In humans, scientists found levels of melatonin to be at least five times higher at night than they are during daytime. Researchers found that they could purposely shift their study subject's sleep patterns by slowly changing the times that they were exposed to light "day" periods and dark "night" periods. After measuring production of melatonin, it was found that no matter how the sleep periods were moved during the twenty-four hour period, melatonin secretion always followed a consistent cycle—being secreted when the subject was in his "dark" phase and suppressed during his "light" phase.

With this information in hand during the 1970s, scientists were optimistic about explaining S.A.D.-like symptoms solely through the melatonin mechanism. But the small group of researchers working on the problem ran into a streak of disappointing results. They hypothesized that if subjects were exposed to light while they were still in a "dark" part of the cycle that the production of melatonin could be acutely suppressed. This had already been observed in experiments with rats. Scientists were chagrined to see no obvious effect in these experiments, which used a rather low intensity of light.

But circumstantial evidence had shown that administration of large doses of melatonin to humans induced sleepiness, decreased reaction time, and lowered alertness levels—all clearly S.A.D.-associated phenomena. This orally delivered melatonin was also shown to deepen a patient's depression. With these results, investigators continued to search for a direct link between problems in the timing and levels of the body's secretion of melatonin and S.A.D.

This has not been found to be the case, owing to the complex interactions of the body's many systems. A number of studies involving the use of drugs to artificially alter blood levels of melatonin have shown that there may be some link between the body's production of the hormone and the onset of S.A.D.'s depression. In some young children with S.A.D., overall levels of melatonin's urinary breakdown compounds seem to be higher than normal. But no definitive link has been made between the low light levels, increased melatonin production, and the symptoms of S.A.D. The best link that can be made at the present level of research is that changes in the level of melatonin are *associated* with the cyclical changes in light and dark but are not the single cause of depression connected to low light levels.

Melatonin has also been found to have a significant effect on cyclical changes in the body's temperature. The human body's internal temperature normally falls to a minimum during the middle of sleep and rises as the time of natural awakening approaches. Any disturbance in the timing or strength of this internal "thermostat" can have major effects on the length and quality of sleep.

Increased melatonin levels have also been shown to suppress the adrenocortical function, which, among other things, produces cortisol, a hormone that is important for energy balance and the regulation of body fat. Since cortisol is important in the creation of the body's fuel, any interference of its cycle can lead to fatigue. In normal healthy humans, the cortisol production cycle seems to be linked to the temperature rhythm cycle. Levels of cortisol start to rise about 3 a.m., peaking at 6 a.m. and then gradually falling throughout the day until reaching a low point during the first half of the next night's sleep. Since the levels build to a peak at the "awakening" hour around dawn, it is suspected that the cortisol cycle is important in preparing the body to face the energy needs of the coming day. Studies have found that patients with major depression have low nocturnal melatonin secretion levels—which in turn may suppress the production of cortisol enough to prevent the body from maintaining the proper "energy" cycle.

The increase in melatonin levels and the coincident drop in temperature levels just prior to sleep seem to be the body's way of inducing rest and conserving energy. The next morning's increase in internal temperature and cortisol prepare the body for the energy expenditure of the coming day. In the S.A.D. sufferer, it is in these times—falling asleep and upon waking—that the greatest problems arise.

Circadian Rhythms and S.A.D.

As human beings evolved within the natural rhythms of nature they developed an inner biological timer called the *circadian rhythm,* which sets the pace for bodily functions according to a daily cycle. As science becomes more sophisticated, we are increasingly able to measure just how the body's different systems go through high and low states over the course of the days. The period of the human circadian rhythm for the sleep cycle—when not affected by artificial stimuli—is about 25 hours, rather than the 24 hours of a calendar day. Troughs and crests in a healthy human repeat and occur at much the same times within this 25-hour period.

Some researchers have attempted to explain S.A.D. as an abnormality in the patient's circadian sleep rhythm, a condition in which the sleep cycle is out of phase with other natural rhythmic cycles in the body. Scientists discovered that in about 80 percent of S.A.D. cases, circadian sleep rhythms have become "phase delayed" so that their bodies feel as if they should still be asleep at the times when they would normally be rested and ready to wake up. Following this line of inquiry, scientists attempted to "shift" the sleep phase of subjects by exposing them to bright light. By exposing patients to such light during the winter months between the hours of 6 and 9 a.m. each day, researchers found that subjects could indeed be induced to bring their circadian sleep cycles more in line with "normal" waking and sleeping hours, with a seeming alleviation of S.A.D. symptoms. But when scientists attempted to show that exposure to bright light between 4 and 7 p.m. would worsen S.A.D. symptoms, the results were inconclusive.

The human body's circadian rhythms not only control sleep cycles but also a number of other functions. It has been suggested that as the days start to shorten in winter, S.A.D. may be the result of the sleep cycle not being "phase shifted" at the same rate as other circadian rhythms. Very recent studies of circadian cycles involved in the regulation of many neuroendocrine functions have supported the hypothesis that these rhythms are phased-delayed relative to their normal relationship with the sleep cycles of S.A.D. patients. The rhythms involving melatonin, cortisol, temperature, and thyroid-stimulating hormone (TSH)—which has direct consequences for the patient's energy level—may become internally desynchronized over a period of time and thus explain both the low energy and hypersomnia observed in S.A.D. patients.

Such influences as work schedules, social activity, exercise, and stress may bump these circadian rhythms out of phase. Not only the period of each circadian rhythm but the intensity may also be affected. The lack of enough contrast between the peaks and troughs of the cycle (perhaps brought on when the stark contrasts of summer days and nights are replaced by the relative darkness of overcast winter days and night)—may not let the body react properly to prepare its systems for changing environmental conditions.

Serotonin in S.A.D.

Serotonin is one of the many neurotransmitters the human body uses to pass electrical signals across the synapse from one nerve cell in the brain to another. It is a derivative of the amino acid tryptophan, which is normally present at low levels in the blood stream. The pace at which tryptophan is converted to serotonin is directly affected by the proportion of carbohydrates a human consumes. As a person eats more carbohydrate-rich foods, insulin is produced in greater quantities. The higher level of insulin facilitates the uptake of amino acids *other* than tryptophan into tissues such as the muscles and leaves a relatively higher proportion of tryptophan to other amino acids in the blood stream. An increased amount of tryptophan can then cross over into the central nervous system and brain where it converts to serotonin.

Serotonin has been shown to play a part in regulating many behaviors, including mood and sleepiness. Serotonin is important in the study of S.A.D. because serotonin-rich nerve cells are found in the region of the brain that serves as the body's clock—a region neurologists refer to as the "suprachiasmatic nuclei" (SCN) in the hypothalamus. Anatomical studies have clearly shown that a tract of nerve fibers directly connects the eye's light-receiving structure—the retina—to the brain's internal clock, or SCN. Because of this discovery, scientists have theorized that variations in the quality and duration of light received through the eye have marked effects on the actions of the hypothalamus. These effects include the timing of hormonal secretions that regulate all sorts of physical and emotional responses such as sleeping, core temperature, moods, and libido—all components of the symptoms exhibited by S.A.D. sufferers.

Scientists then attempted to determine whether insufficient levels of serotonin in the brains of S.A.D.

patients could be the cause of their affliction. Drugs that stimulate the receptors where serotonin acts were injected and found to promote activation and increased energy. This response was exceptionally profound in subjects who had not been treated in any other manner for their S.A.D. However, response to the injection was muted in patients who had been previously treated for S.A.D. This result led to the conclusion that winter's dim light may inhibit the body's production of a sufficient amount of serotonin needed for normal functioning of the hypothalamus and internal clock. Low serotonin levels are also associated with phase-shifting circadian rhythms in rats and may, in humans, interfere with the body's ability to regulate proper circadian rhythms in the low light conditions of winter.

S.A.D. and Human Evolution

The human species has found excellent ways of adapting to its environment over several million years of evolution. But in recent centuries the human body hasn't been able to keep pace with radical new changes in lifestyle. Humans have conquered night, distance, and hunger, but as a result have become disconnected from the cues in nature that continually and subtly nudge changes in the circadian rhythms and hormone generation that keep our internal clocks in phase with the passing of seasons. Current research leads us to believe that S.A.D. may be a result of this disconnect.

The *exact* answer as to *why* S.A.D. comes to be is still a matter of research and conjecture—but fortunately an effective treatment is available to brighten the prospects of most S.A.D. sufferers.

Light Therapy for S.A.D.

Whatever the uncertainties over the exact mechanism causing S.A.D, those who suffer from S.A.D. and the less serious "winter blues" can find highly effective relief by being exposed to bright light on a daily basis. Twenty year's work by researchers at the nation's top medical institutions has demonstrated that this daily light treatment—known as phototherapy—is highly effective in banishing S.A.D.'s symptoms. From its early experimental use in studies at the National Institute of Mental Health by Dr. Norman E. Rosenthal, through the ground-breaking circadian rhythm studies of Dr. Alfred. J. Lewy, to the up-to-the-moment studies by University of Washington's Dr. David H. Avery, bright light therapy has been established as the primary treatment of choice for S.A.D. Phototherapy consistently results in a success rate over 75 percent, and with much lower incidence of side effects than the use of medications.

Enough experimental and practical patient experience over the last two decades has established a number of standards to be referred to in setting up individual light therapy programs. However, since each S.A.D. patient's experience is unique, the standards are only a starting point, and must be modified as necessary in each case.

Light Intensity

The first studies of bright light in the treatment of S.A.D. arrived at a critical breakthrough—the realization that, in order to be effective, light levels must be dramatically higher than the average indoor level. In fact, the first attempts to use artificial light for treatment were very inconclusive until lights with a level of 2,500 "lux" were used. Scientists measure the intensity of light in "lux," or lumens per square meter. Ten lux is the equivalent of one footcandle—roughly the amount of light a standard candle throws off at a foot's distance. So a level of 2,500 lux represents a brilliant light—at least four or five times even the best indoor lighting, or about the level of daylight one half-hour after a clear sunrise. On an overcast day, light ranges above and below around 10,000 lux. The noonday sun on a summer's day may reach well over 100,000 lux. Although daily sessions of exposure to 2,500 lux units for periods of at least two hours showed a marked response in S.A.D. patients, the commitment to spend that much time sitting in front of a light box each day was found too inconvenient to be practical. As a result, researchers at Columbia University set forth to develop a unit that delivered 10,000 lux, which could be used to the same advantage in about thirty minutes every day. While individual needs vary greatly, 10,000 lux has become the standard from which to start therapy.

Duration and Daily Timing of Treatment

At the accepted level of 10,000 lux, most patients show good response after one half-hour's treatment and rarely need more than forty-five minutes per day. Although the initial length of treatment is a matter to be discussed with one's doctor, many begin with this regimen and then add or subtract time, taking into account positive response and possible side effects. While some people will experience immediate improvement in symptoms after just one session, usually it requires a few days for a noticeable change in mood and energy. Over the next few weeks, it is typical for the S.A.D. sufferer to sense a gradual relief from most symptoms until a sustained plateau is reached. In some cases, relief is very quick and almost reaches a level of a "high" before falling back to normal. In other cases the build-up to feeling well continues over weeks and months.

At what time each day the S.A.D. sufferer should schedule his or her treatment has been a point of contention among researchers. But the most recent studies available show that in most cases (about 80 percent) early morning exposure achieves the best results. Most S.A.D. patients have been found to have a "phase delay" in their circadian sleep rhythm. This makes it difficult to get out of bed in the morning and induces a lingering sense of fatigue all day. By using light therapy between 6 and 8 a.m., patients can "bump" their circadian sleep rhythm back into phase with their other circadian rhythms and with the requirements of the outside world.

On the other hand, about 20 percent of S.A.D. patients have a "phase advance" in their sleep cycle. For those people, who get exhausted in the evening and wake well before dawn, light sessions between 6 and 8 p.m. are recommended. Except in rare cases, it is not recommended that bright lights be used after 8 p.m., in that they usually create difficulty in going to sleep.

Some patients who use lights in the morning report that a short "tune-up" session in the afternoon is refreshing. Others split their daily dose into two convenient short sessions. Shift workers and those with consistent jet lag tend to work out treatment schedules on a more trial-and-error basis to fit in with the requirements of their job or travel. In these cases it is critical to try to establish regularity in sleep times above all else. In any case, it is up to the S.A.D. patient to determine just when and how much light works best.

Patient Position and Unit Placement

Light intensity falls off rather rapidly as the distance from the source increases, according to what is known as the inverse square law. Thus, to ensure the proper therapeutic levels to combat S.A.D., the patient must remain close to the light box. Just how far away the patient must be depends on the intensity of the unit and is generally indicated in the included instructions. The accompanying literature will list distances in inches with the resulting light intensity levels, usually ranging from 2,500 lux up to 10,000 lux. Treatment duration periods at each light level may be suggested in the instructions, although ultimately these are a matter of individual choice, in consultation with a medical professional. Since studies have shown that exposure to 2,500 lux may require near or above two hours per day to be effective in the treatment of full-blown S.A.D., the capability of a unit to deliver 10,000 lux at a comfortable distance should be a prime consideration.

It is not necessary to directly look into the light as long as the patient's eyes are at the proper distance from and level with the unit. If adjustable, the light box should be slanted to give the most effective overall exposure to the head area. Many place the box on a kitchen counter, table or

desk and complete work or recreational activities during treatment. Session duration can be easily controlled and measured with the addition of a simple timing device.

Yearly Timing and Consistency of Treatment

Each S.A.D. sufferer, in each locale, in every year experiences a different spectrum of symptoms and different challenges for treatment. Some people are so sensitive to the shortening of the days that they exhibit S.A.D. problems just as summer is fading into fall, especially in northern latitudes where the days grow darker as well as shorter. Many start their sessions in mid-September with at least a short morning period that they progressively increase to one half-hour by Thanksgiving and up to even an hour or more in the dead of winter. As spring approaches, many reduce the amount to thirty minutes until mid-April. For some, light therapy seems to have a cumulative effect over the months that may reduce the need for long sessions over time. Others find a very rapid fall-off in effect and cannot reduce the length of session or even miss more than a few sessions in a row without feeling the rapid return of symptoms.

For a fortunate segment of S.A.D. patients, there seems to be a residual effect of light therapy that may not only last well after treatment ends, but in some cases, into the next year. The need for light therapy may actually decrease—as if the body has "learned" somehow to adapt to the season. While such remissions are rare, some research suggests that by using light therapy as early as practical in the autumn such results may be achieved, even before S.A.D.'s symptoms are visibly noticeable. Vacations and breaks in winter months can affect the course of therapy, as can the erratic nature of spring weather. A minority of patients, due to unique geographical or climatic circumstances, require light therapy throughout the year.

Expected Results

Even though each patient responds in his or her unique way and own time, within a few days, bright light therapy generally induces a sense of increased energy and calm—a greater "lightness of being." A feeling of alertness and resolve to accomplish things may take hold while the need for extended sleep recedes and cravings for sweets and carbohydrates fall off to normal. If the S.A.D. patient is working with a health professional, it is often that person or a member of the patient's family who notices and comments on these changes.

Side Effects and Precautions

One of the most fortunate aspects of bright light therapy for S.A.D. is in the relative absence of harmful or lasting side effects. After thousands of patient treatments, very few problems have been reported. These rare side effects fall into the following categories:

• Headaches, Eyestrain, and Dizziness

During the first few sessions, some patients report a feeling of dizziness or light-headedness. Some experience a mild headache. Others report eyestrain or watery eyes. These problems can be alleviated by sitting a bit further away from the light box or by lowering the period of exposure and building up time slowly over a period of days. Because it is not necessary to look directly into the unit for the light to enter the eye, averting one's head can often be helpful.

• Irritability, Overactivity, and Hypomania

For some, the initial effects of light therapy are so strong that they become agitated and overstimulated, leading to overactivity and later to exhaustion. Mild hypomania (excessive bursts of energy and creativity) occasionally occurs and some patients report they need very little sleep. When and if this becomes a problem, it can be moderated with decreased exposure. In rare cases, where there is an underlying psychiatric condition, such as bipolar disorder, it is especially critical that light therapy and medication be closely supervised by a medical professional.

• Fatigue and Insomnia

When lights are used later than 8 p.m., there is a greater chance that the patient will feel too energetic and jumpy to get to sleep at the proper time. Over time, this insomnia and uneven sleep can lead to general fatigue. Both problems can be controlled by moving the light sessions to an earlier part of the day.

• Dryness of the Eyes and Tissues and Skin Reddening

Since even the best of bright light units generate heat in addition to light, the air near the box can be made dry enough to cause some discomfort to the eyes and nasal passages—especially for contact lens wearers. Humidifiers may be placed close by and artificial tears and rewetting solutions usually provide relief.

Skin reddening in those with fair or photosensitive skin can be avoided with sun-blocking creams and can usually be prevented by selecting a light therapy unit whose lamps are chosen for their low ultraviolet emissions. As some medications increase skin sensitivity, a physician's advice may be required before starting phototherapy.

Long Term Considerations

A particular consideration in research on the effects of long-term bright light therapy has been whether there is any negative effect on the eyes. Although the total amount of light generated by a standard 10,000-lux phototherapy unit is that of a natural dawn, scientists have investigated whether facing the light devices for long periods can harm the retina or in any way accelerate diseases such as macular degeneration or retinitis pigmentosa. Additional studies have been undertaken concerning the possibility of ultraviolet emissions promoting cataract formation. While no such activity has been yet seen, it is highly recommended that all patients have their eye health evaluated by their ophthalmologist or optometrist before beginning light therapy and have a periodic checkup thereafter.

After two decades of following patients using bright light therapy units for the treatment of S.A.D., researchers have noted no increased incidence of skin cancer. Lights used in modern therapy units have been designed to minimize emissions in the potentially harmful UV-B range.

Relatively few pregnant women have been included in light therapy studies, but those who have showed no adverse effect on the fetus. It is recommended, however, that the eyes of babies and very young children be protected as a precaution. In this case and overall, it is simply prudent to use light therapy with care in all circumstances.

Dawn Simulation Treatment for S.A.D. and the "Winter Blues"

Dawn Simulator

S.A.D. and the less severe condition of the "winter blues" are defined as the onset of depression's symptoms during the shortening and darkening of daylight as autumn passes into winter. Dr. Michael Terman, who had been involved for years in research on biological cycles in animals, hypothesized that the gradually increasing illumination at dawn may be sensed through the eyelids in humans and that this may have an effect on "waking up" patterns, as well as on the setting of the circadian sleep cycle.

His group developed a computer system that could be linked to room lights to approximate a natural dawn in time duration and light intensity. The simulation used a feedback loop to closely mimic a natural dawn. But because the brilliance and duration of a natural daybreak varies widely according to latitude, geographical conditions, weather, and characteristics of the placement of the subject within the house, a precise match was not possible. Even so, soon it became evident that "dawn simulation" did in fact demonstrate a significant degree of improvement for S.A.D. sufferers.

Building on this early experimentation, Dr. David H. Avery and his group in Seattle have embarked upon a series of investigations working to further develop information on the mechanisms and practices involved in dawn simulation and the treatment of S.A.D. and other seasonal afflictions. Dawn simulation occurs at relatively low light levels (usually with a maximum intensity of 250 lux). Research on the translucence of eyelids demonstrated that about 10 percent of light at the red end of the visible spectrum was transmitted, while only about 1 to 2 percent of light at the blue-green end was getting through. Even though the lights used in the studies had a predominant distribution towards the red end of the spectrum, it was found that the dim levels of light used were picked up mostly by the rods of the subject's eyes dedicated to the green part of the spectrum. Retinal sensitivity has been shown to be elevated during the early morning, giving further credence to the hypothesis that the body is sensitive to the "shape" of dawn—that is, to the pace at which the illumination increases and the levels of brightness it passes through.

Since there has been some experimental evidence that dawn simulation can achieve the phase-shift of circadian sleep rhythms, as does bright light therapy, this may be one of the mechanisms by which dawn simulation therapy helps S.A.D. patients. Much work has been done to quantify the intensity, duration, and "shape" of the illumination to be used for maximum therapeutic effect. Presently, a low-intensity light brightening over a period of 1 to 2 hours to a maximum of 250 lux is suggested in order to give the greatest relief without causing major side effects or sleep disruption. Dawn simulators can be simply connected to an existing bedroom lamp or to a special dedicated light fixture and programmed to bring up the light level over a period ranging from minutes to hours. This gradual simulation of dawn has been shown to work well in the relief of S.A.D. symptoms, although there have been incidences of brief awakenings and in a few cases agitation associated with hypomania.

Dawn simulation therapy has been shown to be very effective in the treatment of S.A.D., as well as for patients who have complaints of dysfunction in the winter months that do not rise to the level of major depression. For these "subsyndromal" patients, who may not need or want to take the time necessary for daily bright light treatments, dawn simulation is a useful alternative. Since some findings show that up to 70 percent of the therapeutic effect of dawn simulation occurs on the first day of use and it often peaks in three days, this treatment is well-suited for problems associated with shift work and jet lag.

Application of Light Therapy in Other Circumstances

Sleep Phase Syndromes—Delayed and Advanced

Once circadian sleep rhythm researchers established that artificial bright light was capable of shifting sleep cycles either earlier or later depending on the timing of exposure, they began to look for potential applications in the treatment for other conditions. Each human being's personal circadian sleep cycle can usually be considered "normal" since there are tremendous variations within the population. Some people may not suffer from S.A.D., but are indeed enough out of phase with their own circadian rhythms—or with the culture they must live and work in—to benefit from shifting their sleep patterns.

This out-of-phase condition is known as either "delayed sleep phase syndrome" (DSPS) in the case of late-sleeping "night owls" or "advanced sleep phase syndrome" (ASPS) for those naturally early-rising "early birds." Both have been successfully treated by chronotherapy. DSPS is characterized by an inability to fall asleep at a reasonable time and a resulting failure to feel rested the next morning. DSPS has been modified by successively delaying sleep by one to two hours per day for several days until the desired bedtime is established. This phase change seems to hold for a significant period after initial treatment, although many subjects continue to use the light therapy to enjoy the additional benefit of arising refreshed and ready to work. One interesting discovery has great potential application for adolescent education. Studies have shown that many young people who complain of an inability to get up on time for school, and who find early morning concentration difficult may have DSPS and can respond very well to light therapy.

In contrast, it has generally been accepted as part of the aging process that the elderly fall asleep earlier and sleep less as they age. The latest research indicates that the older population does not get enough rest during this shortened sleep cycle and may suffer from ASPS. For them, exposure to bright lights in the evening can delay onset of sleep and result in a longer and more restful night.

In our modern industrial age, production can go on twenty-four hours per day. Shift work and the interruptions it causes in the body's natural circadian rhythms have become critical issues not only for the employee and his comfort, but also for the employer concerned about risk of job error and the loss of critical judgment in workers. Fatigue and circadian rhythm disruptions are the focus of human factors research for airlines, hospitals, heavy manufacturing, and many other fields where alertness may be a life-and-death matter.

Jet Lag

The jet age of long distance and international travel has sorely tested the human body's ability to quickly adapt to abrupt changes in external time cues. Crossing several time zones in a short period of time gives the body no chance to compensate and adjust its circadian rhythm to local conditions. Internal body phase cycles take many days to shift to the new time zone and annoying effects may persist for up to ten days. A very careful analysis of the particular needs of each traveler must be made before light therapy can be predictably used to advantage.

Insomnia

The use of bright light therapy in cases of insomnia is at a very preliminary stage, but is based on the theory that in addition to the timing and length of the sleep period, circadian rhythms also may influence the depth and quality of rest. There is evidence that some people have very shallow cycles—that is, they are not as awake as the norm nor do they sleep as deeply. During the almost constant dark of northern winters and low interior light levels, they develop an insomnia that can be responsive to bright light therapy, which provides a sharp artificial contrast to "reset" their internal clocks.

Non-S.A.D. Depression

Imbalances in serotonin production and uptake have long been associated with all forms of depression. An entire family of antidepressant medications has been developed with this in mind. Preliminary studies show bright light therapy may help to moderately alleviate symptoms of non-seasonal depression. Research is continuing.

Premenstrual Syndrome

Over the past twenty-five years, researchers at the National Institute of Mental Health have been accumulating data on reports that the physical and emotional symptoms associated with PMS in many women seem to peak in the winter months, especially in S.A.D. patients. A limited number of subsequent studies using bright light therapy showed some relief of the symptoms of PMS. Investigations are also focusing on the use of light therapy during menopause.

Alcoholism

In a small scale study recently done in abstinent alcoholics with winter depression, it was found that the use of dawn simulation may be useful in reducing symptoms usually associated with S.A.D. and may even be of use in helping alcoholics abstain from drinking. The research is now only in preliminary stages.

Mechanics of Phototherapy

The Bright Light Therapy Unit

During the early days of experimentation with bright light therapy for the treatment of S.A.D. and the "winter blues," scientists created what were essentially ad hoc sources of bright light using the technology at hand. Designs changed as testing progressed. The first units, used in the 1980s at the National Institute of Mental Health, were heavy, cumbersome affairs that were not meant to move or be used in a home setting. They did, however, contain the basic elements that are still in use today for the treatment of S.A.D.; a source of intense light, a reflective backing to bounce the light out into the room, a diffusing screen to spread the light evenly and protect from glare and possible excess ultraviolet exposure, and a box in which to safely and conveniently contain it all.

Due to rapid advances in the design of electrical components and lamp technology, it is now possible to contain all the requisite parts inside light-weight boxes only a few inches deep and usually less than two feet in length or height. Some more portable designs are not much more than a foot in height or length and weigh less than ten pounds. External finishes vary from utilitarian metal coatings to beautifully finished furniture-grade hardwood for placement in prominent areas of the home. Many fixtures are made to sit on tables or desks for greatest flexibility. Others stand on their own floor bases and these can be convenient for the user who likes to exercise on a treadmill or stationary bike while receiving light treatment.

Early S.A.D. researcher Dr. Michael Terman and his colleagues showed that by slanting the light box—perhaps mimicking the natural angle of sunlight striking the eyes—an increased level of light can be delivered to the patient and in some cases the time of exposure may be reduced. Many manufacturers have thus incorporated slanting capabilities in their bright light boxes. Some units have been designed with wall mounting in mind, while others are designed for travel use.

Lamp Design and UV-B

At the very core of bright light treatment for S.A.D. and other seasonal disorders is the important question of the quality of the light—that is, how widely the light is spread out over the visual spectrum. Researchers, medical professionals, and light unit manufacturers all strive for both the greatest possible relief of symptoms and the highest level of safety. Since the beginning, fluorescent lights were chosen over incandescent lamps not only for convenience, but because unshielded incandescent lights have not been proven to provide the necessary level of safety to the eyes. As a result, most research data has been accumulated using fluorescent lamps.

Studies have shown that at low light levels, the eyes are more sensitive to green light than red. But at the high brightness levels used in light boxes, white light has been shown to be the most effective overall. Current photo therapy units are designed to incorporate wavelengths across the white light spectrum with good representation in the green range. The lamps generally are classified as "wide" or "broad" spectrum with a color or "Kelvin" (K) rating of 4100K. This is the standard "cool" white color as opposed to brilliant sunlight, which falls in the 5500-5700K range. Many designs offer an alternative of 5000K "full" spectrum lamps, which provide a "whiter" light that some users find more effective. This range includes a slight UV-B component that a small percentage of S.A.D. sufferers find necessary for best relief. It is generally recommended that the first-time patient start with a 4100K lamp installation, although there are a number of 4100K/5000K convertible boxes on the market.

The question of exposure to ultraviolet radiation through the skin and eyes during bright light therapy has been a source of intense consideration and research. The UV-A component of standard fluorescent emissions has been shown to be safe in studies across the board. The small amount of UV-B found in 4100K lamps and in slightly higher levels in 5000K lamps was found to have not caused harm in the healthy eye. Those who feel the need for slightly higher therapeutic levels of UV-B in their S.A.D. treatment should consider other alternatives such as spending increased amounts of time out in natural daylight.

State-of-the-art fluorescent lamps used by the best manufacturers are glare-reduced, highly energy-efficient, and have a long useful tube life and compact shape. They are easily replaced at a moderate cost. A high-quality, spectrally-transparent diffuser will distribute light evenly and reduce glare.

Electrical Components

High levels of brightness are attained in light therapy boxes by "driving" the lamps with energy supplied through an electrical component called a "ballast." The intensity of light is in great part due to the quality of the ballast and an experienced manufacturer will always employ the best available ballast technology. Objectionable lamp flickering, heat build-up, and excessive electromagnetic emissions are thus kept to a minimum. Connection wiring and electrical components in the properly designed and manufactured unit must be sufficient and of necessary quality for the task and, above all, must conform to all safety codes.

Sources and Costs

Parallel to ongoing research into the causes of and treatments for S.A.D., manufacturers have been developing units according to specifications suggested by scientists. Presently, there are a number of manufacturers of bright light therapy boxes that meet the standards set by the medical community. These units are available from a number of retail, mail order, and Internet sources. Prices range from around $250 to $600 depending on the features included and the quality of materials. As in any such significant purchase, especially involving one's health, the S.A.D. patient should carefully comparison shop to find both the best features and highest quality components at a reasonable price.

When shopping for bright light therapy equipment, one should seek out a source that

will provide the clearest pre-purchase information as well as a post-purchase warranty and excellent service follow-up.

For the skilled home electrician, it is possible to build a light therapy unit, and many have. But clinicians do not normally recommend doing so. Many of the best components are not readily available to the general public at a reasonable cost. It is often simpler and safer to buy a ready-made unit since good manufacturers have developed equipment that follows the latest safety and effectiveness guidelines.

Light boxes vary in size from portable to floor standing models.

Treating S.A.D. Beyond
Bright Light Therapy

Once the sometimes bewildering array of symptoms that constitute S.A.D. are diagnosed, proper use of bright light therapy can produce dramatic results. However, the very complexity of the condition ensures that no single simple treatment strategy will work in all cases for all people. Since the exact causes of S.A.D. are unknown and the mechanisms in the body working to create the symptoms are, as yet, unclear to medical researchers, it is always best to consider a number of approaches.

While the base causes of S.A.D. are indeed in the physical realm, there is no doubt that the physical reacts with the psychological to create a very difficult and complicated situation for the sufferer. As no person lives in a physical and social vacuum, there are always underlying conditions both of a biochemical and emotional nature that alter and perhaps exacerbate the basic S.A.D. situation. Just arriving at the diagnosis of S.A.D. among all the other possibilities can be difficult enough—especially when one considers that most medical practitioners are not entirely familiar with the factors that make S.A.D. different from classic depression. Frequently, when presented with a patient suffering from some or all of S.A.D.'s miseries, even the finest internist or psychologist can be led off the track to S.A.D. and either offer an incorrect treatment or infer that there is no physical basis at all for the complaint. It is then that the patient must extend himself to take control and help the professional recognize the problem and put together an effective treatment plan.

When cobbling together a total personal package for beating back the symptoms of S.A.D., it is important to recognize that fluctuations in energy, mood, appetite, weight, sleep cycle, libido, and interpersonal relationships are to be expected as part of a natural life. No single or combination of treatment strategies could ever guarantee functioning at peak levels all the time. When choosing possible adjunct treatments to bright light therapy, it is best to work with a medical professional through a number approaches until the best possible one is found. Not surprisingly, it is a rare person who exhibits the symptoms of S.A.D. in the same way or with the same intensity every year. Thus treatment plans must be constantly updated for the best total effect.

Now that S.A.D.'s symptoms have been recognized as having a physical basis, the medical community is at ease in prescribing light therapy in combination, if necessary, with both medication and psychotherapy. Ultimately, a successful treatment plan can be arrived at by a careful and professionally supervised series of trials. Dedication on the part of the patient to stick with agreed-upon treatment is essential.

Environmental Lighting

Since the primary cause of S.A.D. is a lack of light in the overall environment, any increase in light levels, whether indoors or out, is desirable. Light levels in the home can be enhanced in a number of ways. Initially it is very easy and cost effective to survey the existing light fixtures and increase wattage when safely possible. It may be necessary to place more fixtures about—including some that have the capacity for the brilliant white halogen and halide lamps now available. Skylights may be installed in the best orientation to take advantage of the sun's path. "Light pipes," which are shiny aluminum tubes that carry light from outside the roof, can be run into darker corners of the living quarters. Colorful wall treatments, floor coverings, and furniture can help brighten up the room. When structurally and financially possible, the size and number of windows and glass doors may be increased. When buying or building a new home, sufferers of S.A.D. should pay special attention to the design and orientation of the structure in order to maximize natural light levels.

Some research has shown at least a subjective positive response in S.A.D. patients to increased warmth along with light. Patients have responded well to higher thermostat settings, the use of comforters and electric blankets, and warm beverages.

Since people spend so much time in the work place, attention must be paid to the quality and intensity of light in the office or on the job site. Studies have found that most schools and work sites are significantly underlit. The highest quality lighting should be broad or full spectrum with good coverage and low glare.

Better still is increased exposure to the sun's natural light by simply spending as much time as possible outdoors. Morning walks seem to provide the greatest benefits, but any outdoor breaks are helpful, even if it means dashing out for a few moments of sun at lunch.

Since the 1800s, when Esquirol, an early clinician, prescribed travel to the south of Italy for those patients who came to his practice during northern France's bleak winters, the basic way to beat any of the winter's "blahs" has been to go on vacation or schedule work in sunnier climes. Many S.A.D. sufferers plan, if possible, a number of short trips during the winter months as a specific part of their treatment plan. Others choose to take their major yearly break in the winter rather than the summer. While research has shown the obvious—that these breaks do in fact elevate the mood and push back the onset of S.A.D.'s symptoms— unfortunately the effects have been shown to be very short lived.

At the extreme, but not at all out of the question for those who suffer severely, is relocation. While making such a drastic move may be impractical at best, a sunnier climate may ultimately be the best possible solution.

Exercise and Diet

The connection between exercise and the alleviation of classical depression's symptoms has been well documented. Studies with S.A.D. patients have also indicated such improvement. Outdoor exercise is recommended, although indoor exercise on a treadmill, stationary bicycle, or ski machine is very useful when done in front of a light box. Vigorous and sustained exercise is preferred and has the additional benefit of holding S.A.D.'s potential winter weight gain at bay.

Due to the unique mechanisms underlying S.A.D.'s connection to a patient's increased craving for carbohydrates in the winter, diet is a necessary consideration in the treatment plan. Carbohydrate-loaded meals help to activate S.A.D. patients because of their serotonin-producing effects. There is evidence to suggest that serotonin plays a role in creating the feeling of satiety or fullness and acts as a brake on overeating. In a carbohydrate-craving S.A.D. patient, it is thought that the satiated feeling doesn't kick in as soon as in a normal eater and may not be active until at least thirty minutes after the last snack. It is thus recommended that S.A.D. patients eat just a small amount of carbohydrate-rich food and then wait a period of time to forestall unsatisfied binge eating.

However, some researchers have suggested that it is very difficult for S.A.D. patients to eat just a small amount of carbohydrates at one time, and they don't recommend eating a number of small servings of quick sugar-release carbohydrates. These scientists claim that those who suffer from S.A.D. aren't satisfied by snacks as most people are, and in fact these cravings are close to an addiction that is stimulated by even a bit of the substance. They recommend that very little carbohydrate-rich food be consumed for most of the day except during one meal, where at least some satisfying carbohydrates are permitted if eaten along with a balanced meal.

Both of these approaches are based on the theory that carbohydrates promote the secretion of insulin from the pancreas, causing a rapid drop in blood sugar levels. Re-searchers disagree over whether or not S.A.D. carbohy-drate-cravers have a different insulin response than the norm.

A third approach—something of a middle way—is based on a careful balance between carbohydrates, protein, and fat to create a diet that mimics the natural diet of early man. In this approach, the increased proportion of protein to carbohydrates alters the balance between insulin (which promotes glucose storage in the body) and glucagon (which breaks down these glucose stores and releases them into the blood stream). The proper balance can moderate hunger and thus prevent carbohydrate bingeing.

Different diets or combinations of diets have been shown effective in various patients. Sticking precisely to any rigid diet is difficult and not entirely necessary. Indeed, a workable and easy-to-follow path is the best one.

Psychotherapy for S.A.D.

While experimental science has solidly placed the source of S.A.D. largely in the physical realm, many of the most prominent symptoms reside in the areas of mood, emotion, and interpersonal responses. S.A.D. can be a difficult personal trial, as well as a crisis for the patient's entire family. This can easily push circumstances to the point where psychotherapy is recommended. When questions of self esteem are at issue, as they often are in the throes of S.A.D. depression, it may be difficult to draw a clear line drawn between the condition's symptoms and the myriad other influences on the patient's emotional well-being. Sorting out just where these emotional difficulties come from and how they interact with S.A.D. can be hard work best done with the help of a mental health professional. Extended and repeated stretches of depression can be, in themselves, the source of self-image problems and difficult interaction with family, friends, and business associates. Psychotherapy or any one of a number of counseling techniques can be helpful in coming to terms with the situation and, in any case, creating a supportive environment from which to plan an overall attack on S.A.D.

Choosing a type of therapy, as well as a particular practitioner, is a matter of personal taste and comfort. Whether the focus of therapy is for the individual, couple, family, or group should also be considered. In any event, the most important criteria for selecting a therapist must be his or her recognition that the unique condition S.A.D. is present and that a biological treatment must be considered along with "talk therapy."

Additionally, a professional therapist as a trained outside observer can be very helpful in aiding the patient in developing a lifestyle that reduces stress levels—an important step in relieving depression. While life constantly throws unexpected and frequently undesired problems in our path, many stress-inducing situations can be anticipated, and, indeed, planned for.

As S.A.D. flares during the winter months, it makes sense to postpone, if possible, starting major projects and social commitments until a more favorable time of year. Many schedule their more rote and mundane tasks for the months when no great effort or originality is required—leaving more energetic and original adventures for the summer. Advance planning for the unavoidable, such as the winter holiday season, can help lower stress levels. S.A.D. saps energy and motivation from even the most dynamic people. Therefore, it is important for the sufferer to recognize that reducing commitments or accepting the help and talent of others at certain times is not an abdication of responsibility, but a logical and deserved response to a difficult situation.

As focus, concentration, and memory may become difficult for S.A.D. patients, methods should be developed to reduce the stress associated with these activities. By taking care to jot things down and using a rather specific planning calendar, one can both fulfill obligations and gain the needed feeling of mastery over events. Work situations may be manipulated in terms of hours, responsibilities, and career paths—along with the extreme possibility of actually changing careers to where the pressures better favor freedom from S.A.D.'s effects.

Antidepressant Medication and S.A.D.

Research has shown a link between the body's production and uptake of various neurotransmitters and hormones (most notably serotonin and melatonin) and depression. Since the primary and life-disturbing symptom of S.A.D. is depression, it is logical to consider the use of antidepressant medication—under the supervision of a highly trained professional—in conjunction with light therapy.

Once the patient is comfortable with the reality that there is a biochemical and possibly a genetic component to his malady, he or she may profit from the use of a well-chosen medicine to treat the more immediate symptoms of depression. Light therapy can then be used to deal with the overall and long-term problem. The decision to engage in a course of one or more antidepressant medications is a serious one and must be closely monitored. An experienced clinician is able to observe the action of an antidepressant in the patient and assess its effectiveness. Importantly, he can prescribe the proper medication and dosage for any other psychological or physical conditions present along with S.A.D.

There are a wide range of antidepressant and anti-anxiety medications available today, and each group has its own therapeutic mechanisms and set of possible side effects. The prescribing and selection of the best possible medication for each individual is both a science and an art based on the practitioner's experience and on the verbalized and unstated responses of the patient. The S.A.D. patient must create a partnership in treatment with his or her physician and pharmacist. It is important to learn as much as possible about the potential action of the medication, faithfully follow dosage indications, and keep tabs on the number and severity of side effects. Since all antidepressants require time to begin working, the onset of side effects can be carefully monitored. These possible problems include sleepiness, dry mouth, blurred vision, dizziness, and weight gain—but these side effects are usually mild and may disappear within a short time as the body gets used to the medication.

Because the number of medications is so varied and because they should only be taken under direct physician's orders, a discussion of specific medications is not warranted in this book. However it may be noted that due to the increasing evidence that the serotonin mechanism seems to play an important role in S.A.D., it may be worthwhile to mention the family of antidepressants called serotonin re-uptake inhibitors (SSRIs). These drugs have been designed to block the re-uptake of the neurotransmitter serotonin back into the nerve terminals and thus allow the serotonin to remain available to help the nerve transmit signals to the next neuron for a longer period of time. Research over recent winters has shown SSRIs to be quite effective in reversing S.A.D. But these results were accompanied by a wide range of side effects—from the most minor to some rather dramatic ones. Clinicians' opinions vary widely on the use and dosage of SSRIs, as well as on the applicability of other antidepressants in S.A.D. cases. But most agree that a combination of light therapy as the primary treatment in conjunction with antidepressants has worked well in many difficult cases.

Negative Ion Therapy and S.A.D.

Recently, it has been observed that the negative ions produced by special electronic devices have been shown to alleviate some symptoms associated with S.A.D. Negative ions are atoms or groups of atoms normally occurring in nature which carry an overall negative charge. These negative ions are created in nature by the action of the sun and the movement of wind and water. In high concentrations they are capable not only of cleaning waste and pollution from the atmosphere, but appear to reduce irritability and raise the energy levels of S.A.D. sufferers. The normal negative ion count in clear unpolluted air is between two and three thousand per cubic centimeter. In traffic-congested urban settings negative ion levels can fall into the hundreds. A high-quality home air ionizer can elevate interior air up to the five thousand ion per cubic centimeter level, and—subjective reports indicate—elevate alertness and the sense of well-being. European and Russian researchers have experimented with the use of large-scale ionizers in public places and report both an increase in objectively measured air quality as well as a more rested and alert work force. The nature of the interaction between negative ions and the biological activity involved in S.A.D. is not yet clearly understood.

Insurance and S.A.D.

The American Psychiatric Association's inclusion of S.A.D.-associated symptoms in their 1987 DSM-III-R manual has greatly increased acceptance of the condition's physical basis in the medical community. As a result, more and more health insurance carriers and HMOs are covering the cost of light therapy units, when properly prescribed and used in conjunction with professional medical help. Coverage is still very uneven, although providers in traditionally overcast areas and near major medical research centers are most likely to reimburse. While Medicare and Medicaid do not as yet guarantee payment, they soon may. For best consideration when seeking insurance coverage of phototherapy equipment, it is important that the manufacturer and retailer of the unit are qualified as preferred providers under the requirements of the durable medical equipment category. A letter describing the patient's treatment and requirement for a light therapy device sent directly from the physician to the carrier is the most effective strategy.

SAMPLE LETTER FROM PHYSICIAN TO INSURANCE CARRIER OR HEALTH PLAN FOR PHOTOTHERAPY UNIT REIMBURSEMENT

Patient Name: Date of Birth:

Patient Address:

Patient I.D. #:

Insurance Carrier/Health Plan:

To Whom It May Concern: (Insurance Carrier or Health Plan)

    This is to certify that the above named patient is under my treatment for recurrent major depressions with a seasonal pattern. This diagnosis is also known as Seasonal Affective Disorder (S.A.D.) as included in the Diagnostic and Statistical Manual of Mental Disorders (DSM III-R-296.3). I have prescribed phototherapy as treatment of first choice for this patient as described in the Task Force Report of the American Psychiatric Association: Treatment of Psychiatric Disorders, Vol.3, pages 1890-1896, A.P.A. Press, 1989.
    Phototherapy involves daily treatment according to a specific protocol with the specialized bright light unit that I have prescribed. Its use in this case is a medical necessity and is, in my opinion, the most efficient and effective treatment possible. If you require additional information concerning this form of treatment, please contact me and I would be happy to comply.

Sincerely,

Dr._____

A Less S.A.D. Future

Having evolved in harmony with nature for eons, recent mankind's adaptability and drive to subdue the far reaches of his world has led him to the sometimes sad state of being out of phase with his own basic rhythms and subject to the symptoms of seasonal depression. Some of the very biological and physiological characteristics that suited man for so long have now become the source of misery for many.

While most simply struggle with a bit of the "winter blues" as the days grow short and dark, a significant number are truly burdened by the oppression of S.A.D.'s symptoms. Yet it wasn't until recent decades that medical science paid proper heed to the seasonal changes seen in their patients since ancient times. However, once having done so, pioneers in researching the causes and treatments of S.A.D. have applied their own drive and creativity to make great strides in helping patients recognize the reality of their malady. These researchers have provided patients with the tools to effectively treat S.A.D. and have supported them with the happy prospect that things can and will get better.

The symptoms associated with Seasonal Affective Disorder are extensive and complex, and in all circumstances deeply interwoven with every aspect of the sufferer's life. The exact causes and effects will be subjects for study well into the future. But at least for today, the prospect is optimistic, as bright light therapy, dawn simulation, and other phototherapies become widely acccepted as as the treatment of first choice for sufferers of S.A.D.

Along with other treatment strategies and under the supervision of a trained and sensitive medical practitioner, there is no need to suffer silently and alone under the dark of winter.

REFERENCES

American Psychiatric Association: Diagnostic and Statistical Manual of Mental Disorders: 3rd ed rev. Washington,DC: American Psychiatric Press 1987.

Avery DH, Dahl K. Bright light therapy and circadian neuroendocrine function in seasonal affective disorder. In Schulkin J ed. Hormonally-Induced Changes in Mind and Brain. San Diego: Academic Press 1993;357-390.

Avery DH, Bolte MA, Dager SR et al. Dawn simulation treatment of winter depression: a controlled study. Am J Psychiatry 1993;150:113-117.

Avery DH, Bolte MA, Ries R. Dawn simulation treatment of abstinent alcoholics with winter depression. J Clin Psychiatry 1998;59:36-42.

Avery DH, Dahl K, Savage MV, et al. Circadian temperature and cortisol rhythms during a constant routine are phased-delayed in hypersomnic winter depression. Biol Psychiatry 1997;41:1109-1123.

Hyman JW. The Light Book. New York: Ballantine Books; 1990.

Lam RW, ed. Seasonal Affective Disorder and Beyond: Light Treatment for SAD and Non-SAD Conditions. First ed. Washington, D.C.: American Psychiatric Press, Inc; 1998.

Lewy AJ, Sack RL, Miller LS, Hoban TM. Antidepressant and circadian phase-shifting effects of light. Science 1987;235:352-354.

Lewy AJ. Treating chronobiologic sleep and mood disorders with bright light. Psychiatric Annals 1987;17:664-669.

Norden MJ, Avery DH. A controlled study of dawn simulation in subsyndromal winter depression. Acta Psych Scand 1993;88:67-71.

Oren DA, Rosenthal NE, Wehr TA. How to Beat Jet Lag: A Practical Guide for Air Travelers. New York: Henry Holt; 1993.

Rosenthal NE. Winter Blues: Seasonal Affective Disorder: What it is and How to Overcome It. New York: The Guilford Press; 1998 rev.

Rosenthal NE, Blehar MC eds. Seasonal Affective Disorder and Phototherapy. New York: The Guilford Press; 1999.

Rosenthal NE. Seasons of the Mind. New York: Bantam Books; 1990.

Rosenthal NE. Diagnosis and treatment of seasonal affective disorder. JAMA 1993;270:22 2717-2720.

Wurtman RJ, Wurtman JJ. Carbohydrates and depression. Scientific American 1989;260:68-75.

About the Author

Bruce Charles Barr is a businessman and a writer of science and philosophy who has gone to great lengths, literally and figuratively, to follow the sunshine.